I0086531

Volutions

2014 Savant Poetry Anthology

Edited by Suzanne Langford

Savant Books and Publications
Honolulu, HI, USA
2014

Published in the USA by Savant Books and Publications
2630 Kapiolani Blvd #1601
Honolulu, HI 96826
http://www.savantbooksandpublications.com

Printed in the USA

Edited by Suzanne Langford
Cover Image by Suzanne Langford
Cover Design by Daniel S. Janik

13-digit ISBN: 978-0-9915622-1-3

$\mathcal{V}$olutions

2014 Savant Poetry Anthology

Edited by Suzanne Langford

Table of Contents

Bells of Quietus

Spiral Arms

Volutions

Preface

A volution is a whirling, a single turning, or a spiraling motion. There is a difference between volutions and either evolutions (developments, changes) or revolutions (radical changes, revolts) whether they are found in nature or the lives of human beings.

What happens—and doesn't happen—as people interact with one another and their surroundings is the essence of that three-ring circus called "life."

The poems in *Volutions* speak to myriad aspects of existence: a whirl from a hidden core, a turning at a critical juncture, or a full spiral into far-off realms.

Poets revere the written word. Read aloud those treasures in *Volutions* that come packaged in unfamiliar language. The gestalt of this anthology rests on the radiance of the individual poems; each is lit from within. Every word exudes meaning; reaching minds, hearts and sometimes —souls.

- Suzanne Langford (2014)

Volutions

La Magia Della Spirale

The Magic of the Spiral

K. Lauren de Boer is an essayist, poet, and composer living in Walnut Creek, California. He is author of *Where It Comes From,* a self-published collection of 95 poems with a focus on ecology and the human spirit. His poems have appeared in *Albatross, Green Fuse, EarthLight Magazine,* and *Iodine Poetry Journal.* He has published a number of nature essays, most recently in the Sierra Club Books anthology, *Eco-therapy: Healing with Nature in Mind* and *Parabola Magazine.* For ten years he was executive editor of the national spiritual ecology magazine, *EarthLight.*

CAVE PAINTINGS
K. Lauren de Boer

There was the great dark lake to cross.
Our torches sparkled its surface,
Brought forgotten news of how the Sun
has made a habit of hide and seek.
We knew we were moving toward a prayer
That would be rediscovered some day.
We smelled of burnt fat
And only had words for the firm things.
Names had their own lives
that came to us like visitors.

One day this hunch began happening.
A seam of rock stirred into the curve
Of stallion back or spiral of ibex horn;
haunch of auroch grew from a bulge of rock.
We held in our hands
The charcoal from our hearth
And the powder of ochre and oxide.
Fixed with their blood and our saliva.

We stood in the big room
Until some of us began dreaming of them—

The shapes of the above-world,
The herds moving as one body,
The chase and graze and buck,
The gambol and slink,
The kill and dying gasp and first suck.

Then there was the first reach
Or the first blow through a tube
Toward the rough, scarcely breathing rock,
Which received the pigment
Through pores made of light.

Dedicated to all of those who came before me.

Duandino (Duan Kellum) is an educator, artist and life long learner. His writings are often a barometer of his state of being. Many of his works address issues of race, culture and identity.

"Writing for me is a form of therapy. Most of what I write is for personal consumption, but there comes a time when it becomes selfish to keep these thoughts and ideas solely to myself."

BLOOD TYPE
Duandino

Blood that speaks Swahili, Fulani, Akan, Zulu, Hausa, Yourba, Igbo, Rundi, Shona, Kango Maku, Mande and Bantu

Blood that trickles from the open flesh on the backs of slaves, like tears falling down the cheeks of the black Madonna as her son is crucified

Blood, oceans of blood that fall in place of tears from mothers who have had their children ripped from their bosoms never to be seen again

Blood of strong beautiful astute men whose value cannot be measured

Blood of children wailing, lost in a sea of fear and confusion

Blood that has been diluted so that its hues range from peach to midnight blue

Blood from raw cracked hands that created works never to be credited to them

Blood of those who captured and sold their brothers and sisters into hell itself

Blood of those whose faith sprouted wings and flew out of the bowels of the underworld and into the vast free vault of heaven

Blood that drips from my open finger and resonates as it drops to the earth where I can see the faces and hear the voices of those whose lives and deaths have made it possible for me to bleed.

AT THE FEET OF OYSTERCATCHERS
K. Lauren de Boer

She has hidings-away,
soundings-into, frothings-after.
Blue starfish sleep in her hair.
Her coarse love roars
down every shore.

Her deep vents host colonies of worms
waving their arms of praise
on her dark floor.
Beings of light live there too,
etching the dark with shapes of the sun.

One great feast swarms through her body.
Infinitesimals dart,
behemoths ply and cruise.
No far country exceeds
the reach of her birth.
Lick her salt from your lips
and remember your blood.

To know her, I will become an
acolyte of crabs, sidle across

the taut face of wet sand.
I'll scamper at the fecund edges
where life boils over, ecstatic.
My claws will become rosined bows
plucking melodies from the beards of waves.

I will sit at the strong pink feet of oystercatchers
who learned long ago how to grip shore rock
and probe secrets from between the tides
with bills as orange as a sunset.

I will learn to flow into her.
As a disciple of rain,
I'll carry a rowboat on my back,
lovers asleep in its wooden keel.
They'll awaken to her smell,
their ears entangled in the pound of her surf.

As I bow to the flight of pelicans
My heart will plunge too
Down to the flutter of fish below
My limbs folded, my hunger true.

Volutions

Merry Go Sorry Go Round

A merry go sorry is a tale, much like a childhood or coming-of-age memory, that may evoke joy and sadness simultaneously.

Lucretia Leong worked as an English teacher and librarian at several schools on Oahu. Her leisurely pursuits include playing the piano and the ukulele, dancing the hula, and writing. She currently resides in Honolulu.

STILL THAT GIRL
Lucretia Leong

The layering began the moment she crawled from the cocoon,

Where detachment swathed the rawness of being chosen last,

A balm of rationalization was gingerly dabbed,

On those dateless nights when others could not see virtue nor the moon.

Seeking largesse, but a canopy of trendiness cloaked her metamorphosis,

For three score and five, a heaping dose of self-help dogmas swallowed,

 Dispensing positive affirmations to the psyche,

And the loss of husband, mother, and womb anointed by her own father time.

The excavation unearthed the sheathed soul,

Revealing the unadorned girl, playing with dolls,

Unfurling at every delight, still vulnerable at the core,

Proving the imperviousness of the tender mantle of the child.

Homage to Emmy Bridgwater

Suzanne Langford is an educator and mixed media artist who holds a PhD in Education (curriculum and instruction) from the University of Washington. Her professional areas of interest are teacher education with a focus on reading and writing instruction, grades PreK - Adult. Her reading interests include children's and young adult literature; multicultural literature (her all-time favorite novelist in this genre is Alfredo Vea' Jr.); and social novels, either classic or contemporary. Her number one favorite in this category is Steinbeck's *East of Eden.*

JACARANDA CAKE
Suzanne Langford

One
One day in the backyard a young girl made a cake from
the soil and purple petals under the jacaranda tree. While
the cake baked, on the raggedy, red bricks in the southern
California sun, the Donkey, paying absolutely no
attention to the child, or where he was going — because
he had impressive things to think about — stepped on the
cake and thought, "Damn mud."

Two
While the Donkey fetched the hose to clean the bricks,
the child moved the cake remnants from the oven to the
cool shade of the avocado tree. With the help of the Cat,
she retied her gypsy-bells apron, added a bit more soil-
flower mixture and remade the confection. Before
adding six juniper berries she soaked them in a flowerpot
with some happy nasturtiums and the juice of a fallen
grapefruit.

Three
The child considered the Donkey getting ready for a nap
in his miniature beach chair. He was in his Speedo

bathing trunks on the patio, near the guava bush, right outside the laundry room door. She wanted lunch, but remembered seeing only Lawry's Seasoned Salt, Spencer steaks and gin in the house. Hungry for a fried bologna sandwich, she ate a handful of pink guavas instead.

Four

The Donkey woke up around six o'clock, dreaming red wine and steak. Unfortunately, the lady inside the house, who loved the Donkey, was drinking up the gin and not cooking dinner just yet. The Cat announced the good news to anyone who was listening that the child's cake was baked and ready to eat. The girl decorated it nicely with a crumble of wild lupine and put it on the dining room table on an antique saucer. The lady preferred eating at the kitchen table. She served Dennison's chili con carne and corn tortillas and the Donkey pouted because he said that's not a real dinner. Maybe tomorrow the lady would cook pork chops. But the child wasn't listening to the pork chop conversation. She was planning to pack a bag that night, or one night soon, and follow jacaranda blossoms to somewhere else.

Lady Mariposa is Veronica Sandoval, a Chola, Chicana poet who has been performing as a spoken word artist for over 14 years. A Tejana from The Rio Grande Valley, her writing has appeared with Tecolote Press, Aunt Lute, VAO Publishing, and Texas A&M Press. She is a Rio Grande Valley International Poetry Slam Champion, has an MFA in creative writing and is currently a doctoral student at Washington State University. She performs at local and national conferences, and donates her time to colleges, high schools and public libraries as an advocate of education and art.

SHE WAS—THE IMPOTENT SUN ROSE
Lady Mariposa

The impotent sun rose, and breakfast consists of tiny
Twinkies and a glass of juice, and somewhere an old lady
waits for her son to visit. Abuela made the eggs con Pan
Bimbo, and the girl with big chi-chis wore the t-shirt, but
Persepolis ran away and veiled her thoughts behind a
concrete wall. The flowers did not stop blooming for the
girl behind the piano even after she was dead, and she
made sure to put dinner in the oven to be warmed when
her husband got home. Sympathetic ears are always given
to voiceless women, and no one sees as cages are tossed
into oceans, and life was not her own, not her own. She
covered the sun with a finger, uncapped the sleeping pills
and let the worms burrow their own trail home. She let
them walk in the garden, thinning until she was able to
slurp them up between her Venus teeth. She was the
daughter of a mad man who loved flowers. She was a
duchess on her way to play cricket with a queen, she was
every beautiful woman's smile without eyebrows. She
came from under the fifth sun with mango breath, saying
beyond madrina, from under fruit hats saying beyond
your cha-cha-cha.

The impotent sun rose, and she watched the wild boy become the king of things that longed for her. Daisies stood still and watched as she chased cars under the eyes of God, she was naked sapphire, black angel wings. She was busy writing poems, forming government and perfecting agriculture. She was busy freeing the fingers of men, who would undo the binding of her mother's name. She became the stone statue in a black and white photograph found by the bartender that remembered the crazy her. She was the skinny girl on the wanted poster outside the elevator at the train station, she was the Spanish girl that sold bocadillos and coka light at the internet café for 4 Euros. Unable to make international phone calls, lost cholas girls cry at airports as Penelope does and undoes her ugly sweater, because Picasso's dead horses never come with a discount, and lovers left across oceans can always be forgotten. She was what the earth did not swallow, a curly haired girl in an orchid of fig trees, she was morning of green tomatoes, yellowed knees and tortilla soup. She was the hand that held the dead bull's ear, she was the face that the river could not devour.

The impotent sun rose, and she was a story told on sleeves.

C. P. Little (Cathal Patrick Little): I am an English Literature teacher in Belfast. I grew up in a small village in Co. Fermanagh, near the border of the Republic of Ireland. I describe my poetry as a range of reflective poems on family, violence, society, political corruption and the individual.

WAX & WANE

C. P. Little

The back way around the house
was easily the darkest
path that you could ever trod.
Easy to slip on the green glare that gathered
by the wet wooden gate; wood-worm bitten and
soft from a quarter of a century of drizzle.

Yet eight year old cartographers combined
aesthetics, technique and a keen eye,
to map and mark every inch and crack
on the pavement, ensuring that a market go-kart
accelerates, spitfires and thrusts like the SSC;
aiming for a sonic boom down the steep hill
from the play park towards the crooked
weeping willow in our front garden.

My brother told me that
Reilly's cross-eyes, lisp and stammer
came from braking the sound barrier
on the fateful day Old Buddily upped and died.
The thunderous supersonic crack
scared the pulse right out of him!

Grant said he was there too
and it was true.

My mother told me that Reilly was born like that;
to gawk and stare at the poor fool was cruel.

Still, I always wondered what he saw
that made him look both ways at once.

Volutions

CHOIR: OTHELLO, WA
Lady Mariposa

They do not care about the guitar makers
in the City of Angels
or of the howling wolves
playing grandmother's
dance songs
The translation of dulceria is loss to them
and they do not know what it is like
to wear cuetos like blankets

Miss, they can't make guitars
say the brown skin boy
with mayan eyes
Miss they can't make guitars
because they are poor

And with a show of hands
all the brown children agree
everyone in this Los Angeles barrio
looks poor

Poor is the senora who cuts up beefsteak
for the tacos she will sell at her puesto

'Volutions

Poor is the dark skin man pushing
stroller with brown child
Poor are the brown faces walking,
consuming
living

I must pause Rainbows
to explain to the risers
filled with brown children
that there is no need for the world to look like
the display windows of shopping malls

That borigitas always get swallowed by coyotes
who would never hold mountains for borigitas to flee
That 3 generations of guitar makers
make bajo sextos legacy
That to look brown does not mean to be poor
That without knowing and only in 3rd grade,
they will live the rest of their lives
needing to unlearn what
America has silently taught them,

that to be meztizo
is be ugly

Volutions

ONCE
Lady Mariposa

Once my father's hands constructed
    homes for migrant families living on the outskirts of
    the Everglades
Once Native Americans sold dream catchers
    on dusty cross roads that lead to home
Once Christian mothers believed in ancient magic
    enough to know their children's nightmares were
    real

Once my father's hands turned
    the black lettered onion pages of the book that
    would condemn me
    never to be like him or my mother
Once little girls
    locked doors to keep the bad from eating their
    secret good during sleep
Once gliding over crystal cities,
    little girls in glass trains believed they would grow
    up to be princesses in cities like these

Once my father cut his palm,
    sliced till the brown skin turned white,

busted like the plum tomatoes he and I picked in
South Carolina
Once the frog-skinned hands of a wingless butterfly
lost the paper hearts she carried in a bag
Once the pubescent mermaid of a cement pond
let a blue-eyed white boy press up against her
scaling skin

Once my father twisted like copper the wires that formed
me,
told me there were things men were going to make
me feel
and I must not let them.
Once arms that were flesh became the mechanical limbs
of an assembly line,
and no one chased the girl past coagulated cortex
and lobes

Once my father's hands,
shoved me when I refused to let him do to me, what
he did to my mother silently
Apa say it out loud,
say I want to wrap my fingers on your neck till I
drown your voice, say
I never wanted a puta like you, I always wanted a

son

Once while wishing on stars,

no one said, *Wish for more than a cabbage patch
doll*

Once when history made no sound,

eagle-less girls let men build them cities on lakes

Homage to W. B. Yeats

AUTUMN LULLBY
Suzanne Langford

The wind is in the wild
Wood, rain is in the air.
Your summer's gone small child,
But hush, you must not care.
One born the end of spring
Has seasons yet to see,
And each has songs to sing
A babe — asleep you soon shall be.

Volutions

Diapasons

A diapason is an ancient, mathematically-based, musical octave. It is also a full, melodious outpouring and often serves as the directional compass for voice or instrument.

Volutions

ONE WAY TO SING

K. Lauren de Boer

Violin of thrush song,
harmonizing cello of rapids,
and the bass *profundo* of falls,
thundering onto rocks.

Then, contrapuntal
gust of viola wind.

I rest at the ½-cadence of a bench
on this river walk,
a quartet of place
in movements
of dawn, day, twilight, night.

Only just the way
strings make sense of it,
only one of ten thousand ways
to sing the moods of water.

Lonner F. Holden had his first poem published at the age of seven. It still stares out from the faded newsprint of the rural Alaska paper in which it was published. The meager frame that contains it is a reminder of his upbringing in an anything but meager natural environment. He is published in the Marin Poetry Center Anthology. A healing arts practitioner and a father, Lonner is also fiercely protective of the creative process: "I think you can be married to more than one muse without committing bigamy. I never feel more alive than when my conceptual scheme is feeling mortally threatened."

SONG OF SOLOMON
Lonner F. Holden

Come, lie down here with me, naked,
amidst the dewy gossip of thin grasses.
Let me spy, vicarious,
ant's tiny black scouts track
their mission along the ticklish
meridians of your loins;

Watch them measure the advantage
of your peaks, search
vulnerable your valleys;
flee the looming shadow of my
hand to skitter under the
marble ledge of your neck and

Disappear back down the thready
tubes of their cochlear catacombs;
antennae tuned to our breath,
bellows of our ribs pressing slow
drums in on their stoney roof.

Close your eyes. Know
the shadow dance of my hand by its

coolness. Feel the shade of silhouetted letters
cast quill light on your parchment;
the sun's secret language meant for only your
skin, as the serifs and whorls of
gesture recite every reclining
curve you offer to sapphire space.

Beg for the taboo ciphers, quenching cloud
hovering over the greedy membrane
of your blood's thirst, to write your
seraphic visage from the
soft shells of your eyelids -
hiding under the hanging garden of
your hair – to sweep all the ecstatic way
down to the ivory flutes of your toes.

My hand singing, fingers opening and
closing like lips, performs a supple hymn,
yields open your book of love's sacrament;
in soundless tones spells you out,
spired domes to incensed sanctum,
without touching;

Silently signs your name, holy, to
the whispering meadow and the

ancestors of the tree of life
and the tree of knowledge while the dew
gathers us into the nest of morning's
hushed crystalline pillow.

I am, like bees wading too
deep into nectar, drowning in this
pool of knowing the song of you.

Volutions

THE WEDDING
Lonner F. Holden

This mountain is a great watershed -
a heart forged from the marriage
of his deep grey bones,
her high blue breath.

Under the wafting canopy
ancient words have come to
bear witness, to welcome this
man and woman
into the family of wise
boulders and brave wind.

They are heirs to a timeless futility -
of what is not love
seeking its opposite -
of our many weaknesses
searching for our one strength.

Stilled from striving
they stand free to be
seen, to be known.

Volutions

Circumambulating
the same mountain;
she circles him,
he circles her,
exchange rings,
and with one kiss
affirm their ascent
as love rushes down
to meet them,

splashes about their feet -
whispers of a summit
that lives deep within
their hearts;
anoints them with its covenant
in the echo of one
avowing the other's name.

Every aspen leaf and lupine pod
pulse with their union.
Canyons hammer out life as the
blood of loving pours down
freed and wanting,
spilling into the great grail
of the lake -

flourish as cupped waters,
sapphire mirror of heaven's eye -
feeding the world beyond
open ground and billowy dreams.

After "my otter of memory" from *The Otter* by Seamus
Heaney

SEAL OF MEMORY

K. Lauren de Boer

You swam, keeping pace in the surf
while I ran barefoot
down miles of firm brine-wet sand.
You plunged, surfaced, and then again,
were gone, submerged.

What world might I imagine
beneath the vast silver Pacific?—
your sleek mottled body,
flipper-vaulting, tail-ruddering
through paths of kelp forest.

Surfacing again,
wet gleaming head bobbing,
black eyes trained toward me
as I ran
fleeing the bodiless life…

…I know I did *not* imagine that gaze,
which saw me for who I am.
No greater humbling wonder
than to be seen by the exotic other.

Volutions

I ran. You swam, more fleet than fear,
right into this poem,
my seal of memory.

AMA, A POETIC REFLECTION
Lady Mariposa

"...what's wrong with you? The first sky you saw was a Puerto Rican sky. Your first drink of water was Puerto Rican water. But Puerto Rico isn't good anymore! It hurts Ramon and separates my children. So I must be wrong!" (Dolores Iglesia from "The House of Ramon Iglesia" by Jose Rivera)

Ama is that you? Blind remembering Mexico? Mad when I complained my American complaints. My brother wanted a Nintendo, I wanted permission to go to the mall with my girlfriends. You would say, standing next to the brown chimney "Aye, si estuvieramosen el rancho ni jabón para lavarse el pelo tuvieran! Se tendrían que lavar el pelo con jabón de la ropa. Anduveran con el pelo duro duro, y las piernas cenizas cenizas. Anduveran en las calles llorando 'tengo hambre, tengo hambre'." And you would laugh, and it did not matter that we never thought it was funny. Why did you always use that image? Was that you, the little girl without her father after he died on that caliche road? Are you still in Mexico mother? La muchacita who never went outside because she was always sick? Did you sit and stare outside your window to the boys and girls playing? Did you long to be like them? Is that why you can never be too long in a crowd? Do the voices grow louder and louder until you cannot hear your own thought, and is that when you make me pay attention and tell me casi llorando, that you want to go home?

"Nosotros tenemos un terreno en el otro lado," the other side, you call it this, the place of your birth. "Un dia me voy," you tell me, you have been crying, locked in your room. "Voy a dejar todo, y me voy para tras para el rancho. You no necesito nada de esto! Me voy!" You do not need anything from this place; you want to go back to the rancho. You want to be with the images of your father embracing your mother. You want to see him as he was before he died, before the owners of the land he was financing, decided to take back the acreage he had already paid them off for. You want to be the girl before the mother, that didn't have to live with the grandmother that hid food from you, with uncles that fought a navajas y pistolas outside your window. You want to forget that it was you that embraced my uncles and aunts under blankets, that it was your voice that told them it would be ok.

Is it ok mother that I am not like you? That I do not long for the soap-less existence of your rancho? Is it ok that I

do not dream of Mexico? That sometimes I want to kill
the memories of your Mexico so you can be happy with
me here, en este lado? Ama, Apa sold the land to give the
money to his brother; he needed the operation. Is your
Mexico gone? Will you live with me now? Do you still
use the image, tell it laughing to my prima Angela who
comes every day to care for you? Does she laugh too?
Does she know, like I know, that the little girl with dirty
legs and coarse, matte hair is you? That despite the house
with the black tile floor and flat screen TV, you are still
wandering in the streets of Sullivan hungry, trying hard to
recognize the sound of your voice, listening for your own
thoughts.

Volutions

DRUNK ON PARADISE

Lonner F. Holden

This night glimmers with more holes
than the lampooned dartboard
of my disenchantment.

So many stars eclipsing stars
I can barely make out
the decorated sentry of Orion -
I am seeing double
in disorders of magnitude.

Stumbling a sandy salsa,
toes washed by foamy liqueur
of wave's perennial echoes,

breaker's pearly teeth
rip at the undulating carpet
of tropical night's bar -

the water's velvet palette black
from sea swell swirling and folding
every color of tropical day.

Volutions

Bounced for too many drinks of
sorrows sipped at the absolving
shores of sky and water,
I turn inland towards the shadowed
canopy of my derelictions.

Departing this evanescent border
at the edge of what is real,
I do not turn my back
on the darkness -

giddy at this breaking grail
of failed voices
I am leaving behind,
I toss the spinnaker
of my hair out
into spiritous wind

and let the joyous weave
of the isle's sonorous whispers
tempt me even deeper
into the Magi's jungle
of cicada-honeyed dreams.

Born in The Hague, seat of the Netherlands government, **Hans Brinckmann** began a successful career in international commercial banking shortly after his graduation from high school. His banking career took him to Singapore, Japan, Amsterdam, Curaçao and New York. After he left banking in 1988 he lived in London and Sydney until he returned to Japan in 2003, the country he now calls home. Pursuing his passion for writing, Hans now lives in the city of Fukuoka and has published: *The Magatama Doodle*, a memoir (2005); *Noon Elusive*, fiction (2006); *Showa Japan*, a history of post-war Japan (2008); *The Undying Day,* a poetry collection (2011) and *The Tomb in the Kyoto Hills*, fiction (2012). *In the Eyes of the Son,* Hans's first full-length novel, will be published in mid-2014 by Savant Books and Publications.

www.habri.co.uk
www.habri.jp

LOVE IN THE INDIAN OCEAN
Hans Brinckmann

After all this time
The heaving motion survives —
The insidious seduction
Of the febrile body that was mine
When I was a mere eighteen.

Long starfilled, foamswept nights
Bent over the railing, with *her...*
A fusion, sticky and treacherous
In the heady tropical seas,
Passionately desired, yet mortally feared.

The lusting bodies urgent, close,
The whispered compliments an alibi
For deeper, darker instincts,
The mouths glued, promiscuous,
For she was married – but only just.

And all the while the crests and dales
Of great ocean swells mingling
With the pounding of my guilty heart,
Until at last the body, sickened,

Volutions

Abandoned its Pan-like dance

The orgasm finally from the stomach,
Alone, into the greedy sea...
The vomit-stained virginity intact
But the stifled desire more obscene
Than the coupling so chastely shunned.

(London, April, 1996)

Elsha Bohnert is the author of *Don't Trip over the Garden Hose & Other Blood Sacrifices* (Deuxmers 2013). She received the distinguished James M. Vaughan Award for Poetry in 2011 and had the honor of having her work included in *Hawai`i Pacific Review Best of the Decade 1997-2007*. Elsha teaches classes on the Write Your Life techniques of noted film director and screenwriter, Mark W. Travis. She is currently writing a book of stories and poems based on their conversations about his work, titled "Question Marks."

REVELATION

Elsha Bohnert

A phone call like a war club
wrapped with hair sends you
reeling and I catch you just in time
to pull you back into our rumpled bed
our raft through the blizzard
of unbearable dreams

I watch you knife yourself
from the inside out
making old scars bleed
like a rash of startled wounds

Talk to me
I plead
I'm here
come back to me

The night folds in and cries
the shelter of sky rips open and cries
the roads and rivers cry
my arms around you cry
for you

Volutions

for me
for what we know and lack

And when at last you rest
and take my hand
it's a gesture of yes
to all that is and yes
we are the back and front of now
the never and always of love

Fresh drop of blood
my blood
found after you leave
becomes the stigmata of us
the before and after
revelation of joy

Kaethe Kauffman has her Ph.D. in Art History and is an Associate Professor of Art. She has taught at the University of California, Irvine and at Chaminade University in Honolulu among other universities. She has innovated inter-disciplinary team-taught courses: *Art and Writing* and *Art and Psychology.*

FISH SNAP

Kaethe Kauffman

Fish snap and leap in the air grasping for bread slices,
Just as I bite and arch to my lover's rough teeth and
hands.
Delicious bruises emerge from sweet aches.
How could such sting cause ecstasy to brim?

On a narrow breakwater we walk far into the turquoise
sea
Where high waves spit foam on us.
Large ovals of blue-green jump high to grab the yeasty
treats we fling.

How much do I need agony's edge? Why does he inflict
it?
We run to the brink, passion and pain the same life force.
How far will fish fly into a hostile world for a tasty
morsel?

But my habit is to meditate inside the reef, in calm
waters.
After our long walk through choppy seas we near the
beach.

He tears the last of the loaf into tiny pieces, small enough
for the little fish
Who don't battle and jump, but swim in the depths,
patient, waiting.

Now my lover is languorous and lingering.
The fighting fish and the small deep ones share the same
waters.

THE WORMS
Kaethe Kauffman

Deep in my belly, I felt a familiar simmering roil.
Why did I have this ghastly feeling when pleased
To find a stunning desert tortoise shell on my hike?

The Worms, as I'd named my lengthy ailment,
Felt like hundreds of sidling creatures in my lower gut.
After my father died when I was eight years old,
Mom dyed her hair blond and began an endless party;
And *The Worms* started to crawl inside me.
I would twist, trying to shake them off.
On its own, the strange feeling disappeared in an hour or
two.

As a child, I didn't know why they invaded;
I endured their sickening sensation.
Horrid as they felt, they didn't hurt.
Later in life, I learned *The Worms* weren't real;
My inflamed brain induced panic, complete with a ghost
worm riot.
But knowing these words didn't stop the phantoms.

"Oh yeah, now I get it," I murmured as I wiggled my toes
in the hot sand around me.

At every cheerful moment in my life, like the marvelous
empty turtle find,

The eerie phenomenon reared up.
"You don't deserve good things in life," *The Worms* said.

I squirmed as usual when they slithered within.
Dropping my backpack, I plopped on windswept sands
and nestled in;
They gave way like the moist dirt of my girlhood home in
the soggy Northwest.

That rich sienna and chocolate-colored earth birthed
thousands of curvy worms
Who popped their heads into the air after a dense spring
rain.
The birds and I chased and tugged the worms, collecting
them.
Dad beamed when I filled the fish bait can.
I threw extra angleworms in our large vegetable plot
Because Dad told me they toiled hard underground,
Chomping old dead mess, changing it into fertilizer.
In summer, I pulled carrots, plucked peas and green beans
from vines,
Eating as I played, a direct conversion of worm work into
kid speed.

I lay back in heated sand, letting it mold to my prone
shape.
The Worms stirred, as they had for decades.
But they came less often now.
I remembered Dad's garden and smiled.
I let *The Worms* do their work.

Daniel S. Janik is a multi-award winning poet, author, songwriter and producer. His collected poems appear in three published volumes, *Footprints, Smiles and Little White Lies* (Savant 2008), *The Illustrated Middle Earth* (Savant 2008), *Last and Final Harvest* (Savant 2008), and in various Savant Poetry Anthologies and numerous poetry collections and publications. He has authored two award-winning children's books, *A Whale's Tale* (Savant, 2008), and *The Turtle Dances* (Savant, 2013). His pioneering educational book, *Unlock the Genius Within* (Rowman and Littlefield Education, 2005) will soon go into a second edition. *Clean Water, Common Ground* (National Film Network, 1999), his documentary on the state of the earth's water received two Telly awards.

http://janik.yolasite.com

LIST INCOMPLETE
Daniel S. Janik

Straw man, businessman, fireman, thief,
Doctor, lawyer, warrior chief,
Preacher, choir, incomplete,
Dancer, lancer, bowman, meat.

Fat man, rich man, poor man, cheat,
Writer, author, poet, freak,
Leader, lender, borrower, sneak,
Pop star, druggy, groupy, clique.

Policeman, judge, hangman, grief,
Banker, saver, spy or leak,
God and master, seeker, sheik,
Mother, lover, disbelief.

Volutions

THE PEANUT GALLERY
C. P. Little

Suppose you were an idiot. And suppose you were a member of Congress. But I repeat myself.—Mark Twain

No more show-boating, sword swallowing
or anti-gravity unicycle tricks.

An abrupt end to the sleight of hand, wily coin switches
and knotted silk scarves tucked up loose sleeves.

Closed the barn door on the telekinetic king bend,
the dangerous double deuce and the amazing jumping
jack.

A cessation to the smoke and mirrors
and cloak and dagger consorting

with famous friends, infamous foes
and well known strangers.

A criminal, a crook, a pickpocket and plunderer,
a masquerading and marauding murderer.

Volutions

A corsair of contraband, a swindler
and vitriolic hoodlum of the highest order.

We put ties on them and shoved them out there -
right in the spotlight of the opera stage

so we could watch them make jumbo jets
and white elephants vanish in plain sight

and courteously ignore the catcalls
from the nose-bleeders in the peanut gallery.

Borders, fences and seawalls cannot contain the forces of nature. Birds and humans migrate, wildflowers blossom and waves continue to clash. My poem, written in Spanglish, is dedicated to the thousands of deportees who live in "El Bordo" and to the brave souls who work for a world without borders

Noemi Villagrana Barragan grew up in the borderlands of Mexico and U.S. Over the course of 35 years she witnessed the human tragedy and environmental impact of these ineffective and irrational border policies. She is an advocate for immigration reform, a community organizer and an educator.

ALGA FRONTERIZA
Noemi Villagrana Barragan

Fronds dancing aquí y allá

En un mundo de flor marina.

Bordo.

Navegando olas

besando la arena húmeda.

Border.

I am not from here

Ni soy de allá

Muralla.

My destiny es ir y venir

como un seaweed.

Wall.

Volutions

THE WORLD FROM AN ELEPHANT'S BACK
Daniel S. Janik

Once upon a time
A young boy,
Rather a simpleton
(His name was Jack as I recall)
Traded his G.I. Joe Cobra Ninja Action Figure
(Collector's edition - $2,500)
For six fluorescent-colored beans.

Not ordinary beans, these;
Jack may have been a simpleton
But he was no fool.

The stranger,
Who loomed in size over Jack,
Had perhaps
(Jack had to admit)
Too gladly
Traded the shiny new beans
For the old action figure
But the giant of a man,
Hand extended,
Beans sparkling brightly,

Volutions

Had explained they were

Magic.

An hour later,
Jack gathered all his friends
And they held their breath,

Watching

As he planted one,
Then,
Unable to wait,
Two more,
In the shape of a power triangle
As was,
By his thinking,

Appropriate,

And then, again unable to wait,
He planted the last three
Within the first triangle

Inverted

Creating a six-sided Star of David.

God's own pendant,

The most potent magic shape he knew.

They never grew.

Jack's friends,

At first disappointed,

Later disgusted,

Eventually left,

Shaking their heads

At his foolishness.

So

There was no one to see

Him chase down the giant,

And budge, finger and snatch the goliath

And bring home to his mother

The big man's 1942 Rolex Chronograph

And a 30-year U.S. Treasury Bearer Bond

(With 12 coupons affixed)

Issued in February 1977 at 7-5/8 percent interest

Redeemable at full face value amount until 2047.

A local pawnbroker gave his mother half a million for the
watch
(Half of what it was worth, Jack chuckled)
Which she used to purchase and renovate an entire
retirement center
And a penthouse there for herself.

As for Jack,
The U. S. Treasury reluctantly yielded him a cool one
million for the bond
Which Jack used to buy a chateau from a princess in
France.

Needless to say,
Jack eventually married the princess,
And the two settled down together
To produce several rounds of squires and ladies-in-
waiting,
Who ended up growing,
As children are wont to do,
Like beanstalks.

Looking back,
The whole adventure,

(People were calling it "Jack and his Beanstalks"),

Was a fool's errand.

Jack,

I think I mentioned,

While admittedly a simpleton,

Was no fool.

Volutions

MEXICO: YOU ARE MY MOTHERLAND
Lady Mariposa

Por un amor
I spend many restless nights
And I have cried gotitas de sangre
for you Mexico
You have left me with the black and white photos
of dead charros aventureros
and the elongated necks of eloquent movie star
from the age of corrode nostalgia
swept with curled updos
and wrapped in rebozos

Yo no te ofrezco riquezas
And I understand that Mexico
I was born in McAllen Tejas
I was born Chicana
I was born Americana
I was born an American version
of what I would have never become had I been born in
you Mexico
A first born girl,
child to Marin and Esther Sandoval
farm workers en El Centro Campesino

dirt poor then and still poor now.

And when I say I am Mexican I mean it
I ignore your nationalist that believe that crossing a line
for birth disseminates heritage
I ignore your nationalist that believe that I bastardized my
mother's tongue
I ignore your nationalist who believe I have no right to
intertwine the native symbols and empowerment of your
history with my own
Because cholos and cholas are nacos and nacas
gutter trash caricatures birthed once Mexicans
done lost their minds and crossed over to America

Pero para dejar el pellejo,
lo mismo es hoy que mañana

Mexico you do not own me
Mexico you do not own my tongue
Mexico you do not know me
And it has never been about what I mean to you Mexico
And it has always been about what you mean to me

You carry the image of my mother when she was just a
girl

You carry the love of my father on a rancho that would
marry my mother and make me
You carry memories of a grandfather and grandmother I
never met
You carry roots to primos and primas who were my best
friends when I was an esquincla
You carry the connections of a blood line that was
intertwined before the erection fences and the betrayal of
treaties
& whether you like it or not
you are my mother land
the passion that resides in me is directly connected to the
history I have learned from you

Blame it on my mother, she was the one that longed for
you
& her rancho even after they switched her mica for
citizenship
Blame it on my skin, prieta y pobre, lacking the lily white
tones that America covets
I always reached out to you
Blame it on Borderland Texas, because life en el Valle
felt like the perfect blend of the two

El Valle you are the reason why there are no dividing
lines in me
You are the reason why I embrace my mother land and
my birth land
El Valle you are the reason why I am not having an
identity crisis

So Mexico tell your nationalist
que las apariencias engañan
I am not your bastard child
I am not wayward, classless, country less or clueless
I am the hybrid de-hyphenated product of a new creation.
I am Chicana, Chola, Pocha, rasquache,
I am Amerikana, Tex Mex Nepant-lera, Anzaldua~era,
Valluja and poetry spiting pachuca

And if I didn't let America beat the India out of me,
Mexico, I'll be damned if I let you!

IF (UTOPIAN POSTULATE #1)
Lonner F. Holden

If we each displaced our attention from
how another's behavior affected us, to why
it actually did affect us in the way that it did -

if individual focus of human phenomenon shifted
from assertions about how the 'other' offended me
to inquiry about how my 'self' allowed it to -

from the alchemical
murmurs that would ensue -

prisons would transform into schools,
where the student would guide the teacher;

schools would become pure libraries,
where the reader would inform the author;

libraries would become great centers of medicine,
where the sick would heal the doctor;

hospitals would become places of worship,
where the devotee would counsel the priest;

churches would become Heaven,
where mankind would liberate God.

The slave would free the overseer,
the victim would console the perpetrator,
the accused would grant clemency to judge and jury.

Our endless clamor of helpless reactivity
would dissolve into a joyful quietude
of universal complementary engagement.

The politicization of human experience,
and all the oppositions it gives rise to,
would cease to exist, and along with it,

all hierarchical limitations of fear, prejudice,
mistrust, and even the Devil himself.

Volutions

Bells of Quietus

Volutions

UAHI KANAKA
Kaethe Kauffman

Three days ago I sang in Punchbowl, Honolulu's military cemetery.
I poured all my strength into the songs
Beneath the gaze of a 30-foot high goddess, Columbia,
Her arms outstretched as if to embrace me and all grieving mothers.
She was the essence of maternal energy: Pele, Kuan Yin, Mother Mary.
I sang to her.

Today I learn that 200 years earlier, the spot I stood was where
The Hawaiian kings burned their prisoners on a large sacrifice stone,
Drowning them first in a sacred pond at the bottom of the crater
At a spot where today, a Safeway store sits, where I shop for my groceries.
Overcome, I pray that the hundreds of souls who perished on the spot
Where I buy apples and lettuce
Have found a safe way into the other world.

I pray that bounty awaits them in their new realm,
Just as it blesses me every time I enter the site where they
died.

Next, the deceased prisoners were taken one mile away,
Also at the base of the immense volcanic bowl,
For full ceremonies and rituals.
This is today's site of Queens Hospital, the best in
Hawaii,
Still a place for daily prayer, healing and handling death.
Finally, the prisoners were hauled up the steep crater to
the top,
To the sacrificial stone where the fires were lit
To create Uahi Kanaka (smoke of man),
The great kings' gifts to their gods.

Three days ago, I wailed to Columbia with all my power
While Christian priests intoned to their god
And Buddhist ministers chanted the Heart Sutra
While we all remembered the soldiers' agonies
Before they were buried beneath Columbia.

Three days ago, I sang, body quivering
With vibrations so deep I trembled and spit words into
the air.

And it wasn't enough.
I sang louder, shrieking words.
I shook so hard I thought I might take off into flight,
And ascend to Columbia's height.

I learned about the Hawaiian sacrifices today
And yet, three days ago, my body knew.

Volutions

A LONELY END
Hans Brinckmann

Reminders of his roofless stay
Are heaped by the fence in the park
The holes in his threadbare sweater
A sad and painful sight, as are
The worn-out boots, the candle stumps
A voyeur I am, of this pointless suffering
I feel ashamed for not having helped
His desperate plight, seen from my house...

"Maybe he was lonely, and maybe angry
With himself, I don't know why..."
So says a passing boy of six, who'd seen
The homeless man in the park before,
"...and now, in nice clothes, sits happily
On a busy street somewhere,
For in the park he was all alone..."

Surprised, and moved, I have no words,
Then meet his eyes and see his hope
And say: "Yes, he must be much happier now"
It sounds convincing, because I mean it:
Earlier that morning the police retrieved his body

Volutions

Frozen to death, the frost still in his beard.

(Amsterdam, 1992)

I wrote this poem in honor of an extraordinary woman who was taken from this world way too soon. In memory of my French teacher, Madame, who taught me to love history and breathed life into my soul.

Helen R. Davis has a special love and heart for the French and Francophone culture largely due to her beloved teacher to whom this poem is dedicated. She is also the author of the alternative history novel, *Cleopatra Victorious,* to be released in late 2014 by Savant Books and Publications.

DANS LA MEMOIRE DE MADAME
Helen R. Davis

She taught me French, faith
And to write of queens and kings.
Madame was my teacher,
I knew her only a year.

When I nearly unsigned my soul
Elle m'a envoyé une carte de voeux special.
Madame as my angel,
Signed me in again.

While Madame succumbed I feigned strength.
Je lui ai envoyé une de ses cartes de vœux favoris
Madame was mon amie,
"Rock, ciseaux... papier." I exhaled.

Madame is their teacher,
Anges dans l'étude du ciel.
Madame était mon professeur;
I write histoires de reines.

In further thought of **Milton's** *Paradise Lost*.

UNLIKE THE PLACE FROM WHENCE THEY FELL

C. P. Little

He got the 77a. They know that.
And had 'Thuban' tattooed on his wrist.
And sat slumped on the fold down disabled seat.
And stared at the nodding trainee nurse.
And sniffed a lot. And wiped his nose on his palm.
And cleared his throat and spat at his feet,
near Mrs Black's brown work satchel.

They know he got off when the bus stopped
and walked carrying invisible carpets.
And ignored the red man
and a yelling bellow from a Volvo.
And looked at himself in an Oxfam window.
And traced his eyes along the shop assistant
as she reached to a high shelf for this or that.

They know he moved down the hill
and into the rank fog and skid-marked snow
of the coldest night in twenty-seven years,
ignoring the orange glow of the fluorescent lights
that kissed the spitting drizzle

and made it dance like the stars
above the swelling North Sea in November.

INTERSTATE FIVE SOUTH
Suzanne Langford

Five North, past the Inland Empire, a golden lonely
    highway
Ninety miles an hour to nowhere or somewhere, just
    choose the right lane
Then it's Mill Valley, to You. Me sadder than the sorry
    country songs drifting through
Miles of radio, forlorn rest stop restrooms, please god a
    Starbucks and gas pump stores
I drive too fast and feel one with the truckers hauling
    heavy, hidden loads

After morphine, Ativan, and hospice nurses left you for
    someone else;
And your husband left you the other half of his heart;
You left your—Jesus!—dead, baby-down-chickie-head
    lying sideways on the pillow.

Three women prayed as many more
We washed ritually knowing words for nothing Holy
We held hands and sipped honeyed tea
To drown the strangled death sounds
And slake our own lusty appetites for life

Where are you who loved your breasts and whorish,
    turquoise panties?
Where are you baby sister…now newborn-dead in

hospice-issued diapers?
Shit, the bladder. Please…we tried your panties…forgive
    us?

Three women murmured as angels,
We lit candles and kindled a softer, warmer dark to dress
    your body
Though you radiated doomed departure despite artfully
    graced flowers,
"Just so," beneath your chin. All dressed up and nowhere
    to go,
Ordained and hopeless as Waterhouse's Ophelia.

Then, hovering over your exit-stage-nothing-left hospital
    bed,
Over the leftover Chux, disposables, under-pads, and
    excess "end-of-life, for your loved one; your Hospice
    nurse can advise you in this" rubble…you circled
    higher,
Freed but still fouled. Do something, you begged, or was
    it us?

Three women hurled your Mr. live-in lover, Prince of
    Pain's shit to the night
Sent it soaring off the deck: scaring deer, smashing stars,
    scattering all to heaven and
Shifting the space for approaching bay winds, devout and
    darkening.
Shivering, as gentle gusts cleansed and carried you in
    their mid-May chill we whispered,

"Hey, you have a two-way ticket to ride, don't you?"

Your body was cold, curled, and fetal—eerily endowed.
You'd left.
The hearse came the next day. I seep primordial tears
    whenever the wind stirs.
You aren't there; that's the fucking problem.

Five South is a golden lonely highway.

Leilani Madison (Elaine Zablotny Madison) received her Ph. D. in English from Yale University and taught at colleges in the New York City area before moving to the island of Oahu where she taught world literature at Hawaii Pacific University. Her first name transformed into Leilani when she began to dance the hula. Poetry is her first love. She is currently completing a memoir.

LULLABY FOR MY MOTHER AT 103
Leilani Madison

Good bye, my darling, choose to trust
Last leaves all flutter down to earth
Release and go the way we must

We raise our heads for oil-blessed dust
You raised us well around your hearth
Good bye, my darling, choose to trust

We grew, we left, we will adjust
Your absence will not be our death
Release and go the way we must

We changed no matter how you fussed
Cling no more to the rights of birth
Good bye, my darling, choose to trust

Forgive me if I was unjust
You gave me love, I know my worth
Release and go the way we must

And now, my mother, abandon lust
For life, this life, another breath

Volutions

Good bye, my darling, choose to trust
Release and go the way we must

UPON DYING
Lonner F. Holden

Breathe in and you rise, warm music,
into accepting. Darkness,
the mystery whispers your name. As your first breath,
it matters that you are witnessed
into accepting darkness.
Stay, focus to a single point, become shadow.
It matters that you are witnessed
up in limitless height where knowing wakes.
Stay, focus to a single point. Become shadow,
find your circle there. Remember where it had appeared
up in limitless height, where knowing wakes
hosts of angels. Hymn your future.
Find your circle there, remember where it had appeared.
Black nakeds you. In innocence
hosts of angels hymn your future.
Forget the world, it dies beneath you
black, nakeds you in innocence.
Abandon sense and feel Everything. Stop,
forget the world, it dies beneath you.
You are unimportant. As everything,
abandon sense and feel everything stop.
The mystery whispers your name as your first breath.

You are unimportant as everything.
Breathe in and you rise warm music.

Volutions

Spiral Arms

The long, winding arms of spiral galaxies, like the Milky Way, are the areas where the newest, and brightest stars are forming.

Volutions

COMING ALIVE
Leilani Madison

Glass gecko
Poised, elastic
One foot lifted, waiting
Head flattened
Sliding beneath my finger

Do you yearn
To slip your crystal form
To slither loose and free
Slurping the rain
Immersed, translucent
Your innards showing
Throbbing
Your whole body
One rapid pulse
Of reptile life?

Trust me now
In your terror
I hold you in my hands
I'll let you go
Into the wild world

Volutions

Where you belong

AWAKENING

K. Lauren de Boer

The sun bathes the bare stalks
bakes out the sprouts
and smells of earth ripening
from the boggy meadow.

From beneath the wind's net
a quail call sails. The rush
of the stream comes
coaxing, up from the valley.

The trees slough off
the hardy hold of winter,
laughing from inside
their bark. So the hour's

come round again
when the emissaries of life awaken,
cross the threshold
into the dream of spring

and I stand captive,
speechless, still, and again.

Thanks to Dr. Jeanne S. M. Willette for inspiration and to Sandra Finney and Loke Simon who collaborated with me in writing the first three lines.

This poem is dedicated to Suzanne Langford with gratitude for encouraging collaborative writing in her course, "Narrative Collage and Surrealist Voices."

NEW SURREALIST VOICE SINGING
Leilani Madison

The phoenix arose, alienated and uncertain, from ground zero, mute testimony to the destruction of the fleeting world.

Leaving the shattered lands, searching for purpose in her next life, the phoenix asked, "Am I going to do the whole thing all over again? Arise and go, fly across the sky, find a mate, procreate, nest—and then conflagrate? Is that all there is?"

Posing this question, the phoenix set off in search of an alternative future. She chose not to procreate, not to lay an egg as she always had in past incarnations. She felt oddly free and definitely untethered. She had slipped off the wheel of eternal return and was sailing into uncharted territory. Images of Icarus haunted her eyes but undaunted she flew on.

Gradually, the cosmos began to expand and invited her to slip between the worlds. Far below she saw the old world with its new ground zero preparing to incinerate itself.

From a distance, it was so beautiful—the great work of destruction I refused to join, she mused. "I simply am," she sang and soared, "I am, I am, I am."

MEDITATION
Kaethe Kauffman

I bounce in a gust of air.
Between drafts, I float and wander.
Light and airy, my molecules drift apart.
I let them separate, each one an entity.
It's okay to disassemble,
To trust the air to hold me,
To trust the wind to direct me,
To trust my mind to disappear,
To trust my atoms to vibrate,
Not knowing where they go.
But when my tiny parts reassemble,
I will be changed.

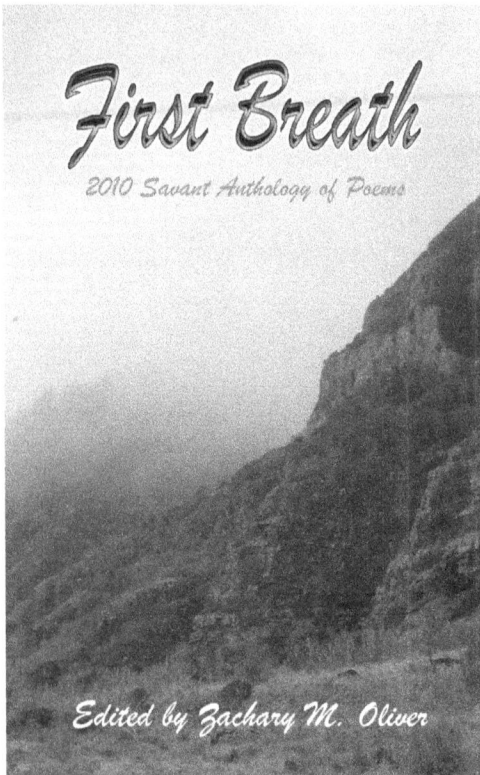

First Breath - 2010 Savant Anthology of Poems (2010)
Zachary M. Oliver (Editor)
72 pp. 5.25" x 8" Softcover
ISBN 978-0-9845552-2-2

Twenty-nine poems by ten outstanding poets and writers
selected for their outstanding merit, including Helen Doan,
Erin L. George, Jack Howard, Daniel S. Janik, Scott Mastro,
Zachary M. Oliver, Francis H. Powell, Gabjirel Ra, V. Bright
Saigal and Orest Stocco.

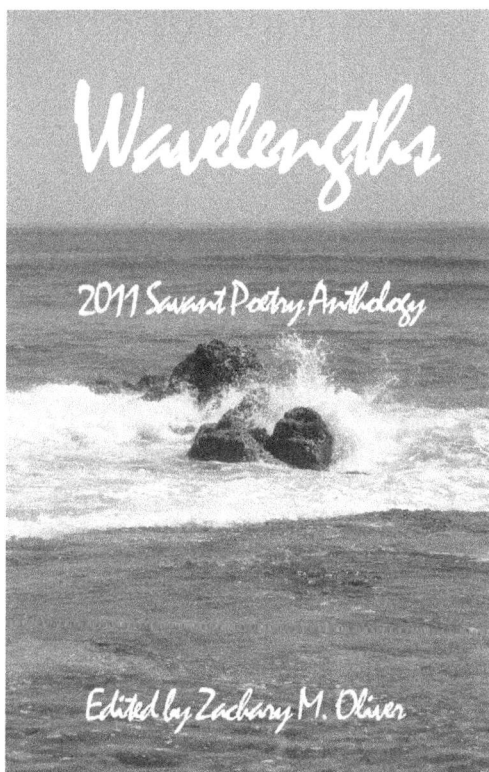

Wavelengths - 2011 Savant Poetry Anthology (2011)
Zachary M. Oliver (Editor)
102 pp. 5.25" x 8" Softcover
ISBN 978-0-9829987-6-2

*Thirty-eight poems by sixteen outstanding poets and writers
including Four Arrows, Penny Lynn Cates, J. R. Coleman,
Nadia Cox, Helen Doan, Erin L George, IKO, Daniel S. Janik,
Vivekanand Jha, A. K. Kelly, Zachary M. Oliver, Cara
Richardson, Michael Shorb, Jason Sturner, Jean Yamasaki
Toyama and Jeremy Ussher.*

LONDON BOOK FESTIVAL AWARD

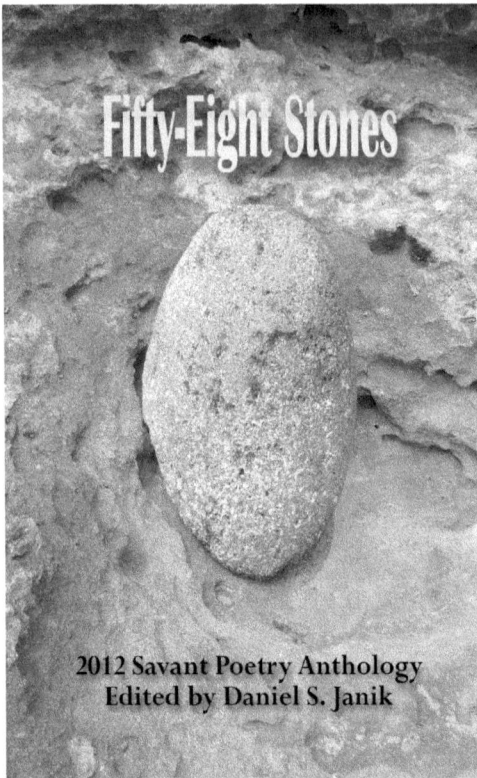

Fifty-Eight Stones - 2012 Savant Poetry Anthology (2012)
Daniel S. Janik (Editor)
128 pp. 5.25" x 8" Softcover
ISBN 978-0-9852506-5-2

Thirty-four outstanding poems by eleven exceptional and many award-winning poets including Shawn Canon, Nadia Cox, Helen Doan, David Gemmell, Richard Hookway, Daniel S. Janik, Vivekanand Jha, Doc Krinberg, Julie McKinney, Francis Powell and Jean Yamasaki Toyama.

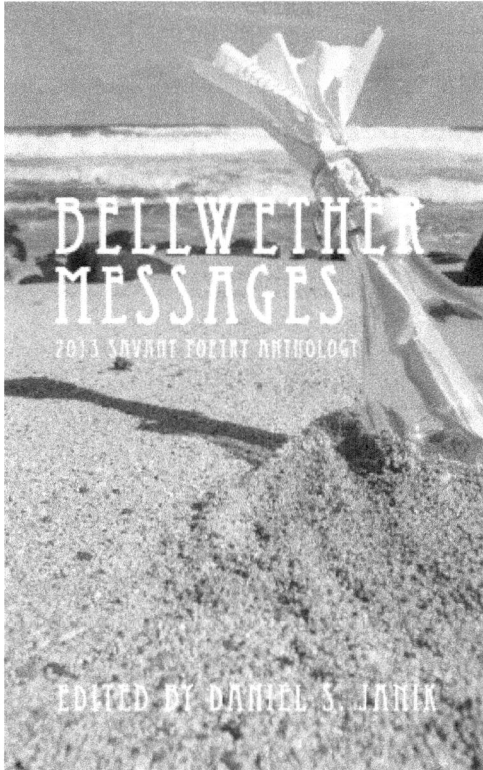

Bellwether Messages - 2013 Savant Poetry Anthology (2013)

Daniel S. Janik (Editor)

134 pp. 5.25" x 8" Softcover Pocketbook

ISBN 978-0-9886640-4-3

Thirty-two selected poems by fourteen outstanding poets including Tender Bastard, Shawn P. Canon, Natascha Hoover, IKO, Daniel S. Janik, Vivekanand Jha, Thomas Koron, Doc Krinberg, Cathal Patrick Little, Peter Mallett, Emma Myles, Ken Rasti, Uhene' and Ashley Vaughan.

LONDON BOOK FESTIVAL AWARD

Other Works by this Publisher

If you enjoyed *Volutions,* consider these other fine works from Savant Books and Publications:

Savant Poetry Anthologies:
First Breath (2010) edited by Z. M. Oliver
Wavelengths (2011) edited by Zachary M. Oliver
Fifty-Eight Stones (2012) edited by Daniel S. Janik
Bellwether Messages (2013) edited by Daniel S. Janik

Other Savant Poetry Collections:
Footprints, Smiles and Little White Lies by Daniel S. Janik
The Illustrated Middle Earth by Daniel S. Janik
Last and Final Harvest by Daniel S. Janik

Other Savant Books and Publications:
Essay, Essay, Essay by Ysuo Kobachi
A Whale's Tale by Daniel S. Janik
Tropic of California by R. Page Kaufman
Tropic of California (the companion music CD) by R. Page Kaufman
The Village Curtain by Tony Tame
Dare to Love in Oz by William Maltese
The Interzone by Tatsuyuki Kobayashi
Today I Am a Man by Larry Rodness
The Bahrain Conspiracy by Bentley Gates
Called Home by Gloria Schumann
Kanaka Blues by Mike Farris
Poor Rich by Jean Blasiar
The Jumper Chronicles - Quest for Merlin's Map by W. C. Peever
William Maltese's Flicker by William Maltese
My Unborn Child by Orest Stocco
Last Song of the Whales by Four Arrows
Perilous Panacea by Ronald Klueh
Falling but Fulfilled by Zachary M. Oliver
Mythical Voyage by Robin Ymer
Hello, Norma Jean by Sue Dolleris
Richer by Jean Blasiar
Manifest Intent by Mike Farris

Charlie No Face by David B. Seaburn
Number One Bestseller by Brian Morley
My Two Wives and Three Husbands by S. Stanley Gordon
In Dire Straits by Jim Currie
Wretched Land by Mila Komarnisky
Chan Kim by Ilan Herman
Who's Killing All the Lawyers? by A. G. Hayes
Ammon's Horn by G. Amati
Almost Paradise by Laurie Hanan
Communion by Jean Blasiar and Jonathan Marcantoni
The Oil Man by Leon Puissegur
Random Views of Asia from the Mid-Pacific by William E. Sharp
The Isla Vista Crucible by Reilly Ridgell
Blood Money by Scott Mastro
In the Himalayan Nights by Anoop Chandola
Rules of Privilege by Mike Farris
On My Behalf by Helen Doan
Traveler's Rest by Jonathan Marcantoni
Keys in the River by Tendai Mwanaka
Chimney Bluffs by David B. Seaburn
The Loons by Sue Dolleris
The Judas List by A. G. Hayes
Path of the Templar - Book Two of The Jumper Chronicles by W. C. Peever
Shutterbug by Buz Sawyers
The Desperate Cycle by Tony Tame
Blessed are the Peacekeepers by Tom Donnelly and Mike Munger
Purple Haze by George B. Hudson
The Turtle Dances by Daniel S. Janik
The Lazarus Conspiracies by Richard Rose
Imminent Danger by A. G. Hayes
Lullaby Moon (CD) by Malia Elliott

Soon to be Released:
The Hanging of Dr. Hanson by Bentley Gates
Flight of Destiny by Francis Powell
In the Eyes of the Son by Hans Brinckmann
www.savantbooksandpublications.com

www.ingramcontent.com/pod-product-compliance
Lightning Source LLC
Chambersburg PA
CBHW072005060426
42446CB00042B/1834